In
1935 if you wanted to
read a good book, you needed
either a lot of money or a library card.
Cheap paperbacks were available, but their
poor production generally mirrored the quality
between the covers. One weekend that year,
Allen Lane, Managing Director of The Bodley Head,
having spent the weekend visiting Agatha Christie,
found himself on a platform at Exeter station trying to
find something to read for his journey back to London.
He was appalled by the quality of the material he had to
choose from. Everything that Allen Lane achieved from that
day until his death in 1970 was based on a passionate belief
in the existence of 'a vast reading public for intelligent
books at a low price'. The result of his momentous vision
was the birth not only of Penguin, but of the 'paperback
revolution'. Quality writing became available for the price of
a packet of cigarettes, literature became a mass medium
for the first time, a nation of book-borrowers became a
nation of book-buyers – and the very concept of book
publishing was changed for ever. Those founding
principles – of quality and value, with an overarching
belief in the fundamental importance of reading –
have guided everything the company has
done since 1935. Sir Allen Lane's
pioneering spirit is still very much alive
at Penguin in 2005. Here's to
the next 70 years!

MORE THAN A BUSINESS

'We decided it was time to end the almost customary half-hearted manner in which cheap editions were produced – as though the only people who could possibly want cheap editions must belong to a lower order of intelligence. We, however, believed in the existence in this country of a vast reading public for intelligent books at a low price, and staked everything on it'
Sir Allen Lane, 1902–1970

'The Penguin Books are splendid value for sixpence, so splendid that if other publishers had any sense they would combine against them and suppress them'
George Orwell

'More than a business … a national cultural asset'
Guardian

'When you look at the whole Penguin achievement you know that it constitutes, in action, one of the more democratic successes of our recent social history'
Richard Hoggart

1914: *Why the World Went to War*

NIALL FERGUSON

PENGUIN BOOKS

PENGUIN BOOKS

Published by the Penguin Group
Penguin Books Ltd, 80 Strand, London WC2R ORL, England
Penguin Group (USA) Inc., 375 Hudson Street, New York, New York 10014, USA
Penguin Group (Canada), 10 Alcorn Avenue, Toronto, Ontario, Canada M4V 3B2
(a division of Pearson Penguin Canada Inc.)
Penguin Ireland, 25 St Stephen's Green, Dublin 2, Ireland
(a division of Penguin Books Ltd)
Penguin Group (Australia), 250 Camberwell Road, Camberwell, Victoria 3124,
Australia (a division of Pearson Australia Group Pty Ltd)
Penguin Books India Pvt Ltd, 11 Community Centre,
Panchsheel Park, New Delhi – 110 017, India
Penguin Group (NZ), cnr Airborne and Rosedale Roads, Albany,
Auckland 1310, New Zealand (a division of Pearson New Zealand Ltd)
Penguin Books (South Africa) (Pty) Ltd, 24 Sturdee Avenue,
Rosebank 2196, South Africa

Penguin Books Ltd, Registered Offices: 80 Strand, London WC2R ORL, England

www.penguin.com

The Pity of War first published by Allen Lane 1998
This adapted extract published as a Pocket Penguin 2005

1

Set in 11/13pt Monotype Dante
Typeset by Palimpsest Book Production Limited
Polmont, Stirlingshire
Printed in England by Clays Ltd, St Ives plc

*Die unwahrscheinlichsten Gespräche, die hier
geführt werden, sind wörtlich gesprochen worden;
die grellsten Erfindungen sind Zitate.*

Karl Kraus, *The Last Days of Mankind*

('The most improbable conversations you will find here
were actually spoken verbatim; what seem the most frightful inventions are in fact quotations.')

Introduction

When the statesmen who took Europe to war in 1914 came to write their memoirs, they agreed on one thing: the war had been inevitable – the result of such vast historical forces that no human agency could have prevented it. 'The nations slithered over the brink into the boiling cauldron of war,' wrote David Lloyd George in a famous passage in his *War Memoirs*. Nor was this the only metaphor he employed to convey the vast, impersonal forces at work. The war was a 'cataclysm', a 'typhoon' beyond the control of the statesmen. As Big Ben struck 'the most fateful hour' on 4 August, it 'echoed in our ears like the hammer of destiny . . . I felt like a man standing on a planet that had been suddenly wrenched from its orbit . . . and was spinning wildly into the unknown'. Winston Churchill used the same astronomical image in his *World Crisis*:

One must think of the intercourse of nations in those days . . . as prodigious organizations of forces . . . which, like planetary bodies, could not approach each other in space without . . . profound magnetic reactions. If they got too near the lightnings would begin to flash, and beyond a certain point they might be attracted altogether from the orbits . . . they were [in] and draw each other into due collision.

Climatic images were also popular. Like Churchill, who remembered 'a strange temper in the air', Sir Edward Grey laid part of the blame on the 'miserable and unwholesome atmosphere'.

The appeal, to the politicians who had made the war, of all these images of natural catastrophe is easy to explain. At a time when the war had come to be seen as the greatest calamity of modern times, they lent credibility to the politicians' claim that it had been beyond their power to prevent it. Grey stated quite explicitly that the war had been 'inevitable'. Indeed, he expressed this view as early as May 1915, when he admitted that 'one of his strongest feelings' during the July Crisis had been 'that he himself had no power to decide policy'. 'I used to torture myself,' he admitted in April 1918, 'by questioning whether by foresight or wisdom I could have prevented the war, but I have come to think no human individual could have prevented it.' Theobald von Bethmann Hollweg, the German Chancellor in 1914, had used similar words just two months before: 'Again and again I ask myself if it could have been avoided and what I should have done differently.' Needless to say, he could think of nothing. In the words of the Chief of the Austrian General Staff, Conrad von Hötzendorf, 'the catastrophe of the world war came almost inevitably and irresistibly.'

By examining closely what all these men did in the decisive days of 1914 – what the Viennese satirist Karl Kraus later called 'The Last Days of Mankind' – I attempt to challenge these self-serving and deterministic claims and to show that the First World War, far from being some kind of natural disaster, was the catastrophic result of defective decisions.

Why Bosnia?

At root, the outbreak of the First World War in 1914 was the most explosive of all the possible answers to the 'Eastern Question'. That question was simple enough: after the Ottoman Empire had been largely driven out of Europe, who should dominate the Balkans? It was a question inseparable from the region's religious and ethnic divisions. But above all it was a question of great power politics.

For most of the nineteenth century, Russia had been the most assertive of the powers interested in the region, with Austria its perennial but much distracted rival. Britain and France were more likely to side with the latter than the former. The 'Near East' (unlike the 'Middle' and 'Far' variants, the phrase has fallen into disuse) was a convenient place for naval war – nothing was easier for the British fleet than to chug along from Malta to the Dardanelles – though an unhealthy place for soldiering, as all concerned discovered at Sebastopol in 1854–5 and again at the other end of the Black Sea sixty years later. The Russians were reminded of this in 1877, when their advance towards Constantinople ground to a halt at Plevna, thereby averting the need for a Second Crimean War.

Throughout the nineteenth century Prussia and then Germany played almost no part in this drama. Bismarck wisely preserved the bones of his Pomeranian grenadiers for use in more northerly climes. At the turn of the century, however, there was a realignment. In the absence of a serious Russian naval presence in the Black Sea, Britain was paying less attention to the hoary old issue of control of the Straits. Germany, on the other hand, had begun to take an economic and political interest in Turkey, symbolized by the projected Berlin–Baghdad railway. Perhaps most importantly, the Balkan states that had acquired (or been given) independence from Ottoman rule in the nineteenth century began to pursue policies which were at once more aggressive and more autonomous. In 1886 it had been possible for Russia to kidnap Prince Alexander of Bulgaria when he showed signs of pursuing a policy of his own (even when the policy was not so different from Russia's own of creating a 'big Bulgaria'). The government of Serbia, however, was never so subject to St Petersburg, and its policy was aggressively nationalist and expansionist. What Greece had done in the Peloponnese in the 1820s, what Belgium had done in Flanders in the

1830s, what Piedmont had done in Italy in the 1850s and what Prussia had done in Germany in the 1860s – that was what the Serbs wanted to do in the Balkans in the 1900s: to extend their territory in the name of nationalism.

The success or failure of small states to achieve independence or enlargement always hinged, however, on the constellation of great power politics. It was the balance, or lack of balance, between Leopold von Ranke's 'pentarchy' of great powers that mattered. Thus the Greeks and Serbs were (partially) successful against the Turks in the 1820s only as far as the powers allowed them to be. Typical of the way new states were created was the 1830 international agreement that turned Greece into a tame monarchy with a German king. The same thing happened in the 1830s when the Belgians broke away from the Dutch; it was only in 1839 that the conflicting interests of the great powers were harmonized in the fateful agreement neutralizing the new state. The creation of Rumania out of the provinces of Moldavia and Wallachia in 1856 – the only lasting consequence of the Crimean imbroglio – was another case.

Piedmont and Prussia, by contrast, were the beneficiaries of international disagreement and disinterest. Cavour got his North Italian confederation with the support of Napoleon III; the subsequent acquisition of the papal states, Naples and Sicily was one of the rare occasions when the few real nationalists – in the form of Garibaldi's Thousand – won the day. Prussia created the German Reich partly by defeating Denmark, Austria and France, mainly because Britain and Russia had no objection. Bulgarian independence was a Russian project scaled down by British threats of intervention: hence the short-lived Ruritanian statelet Eastern Rumelia and the continuation of Ottoman rule in Macedonia. Later, Norway won independence from Sweden without anyone else minding. It was a sign of how far nationalism's revolutionary potential went unfulfilled that all the new states were monarchies, and most of the new thrones were filled by scions of the established royal houses. Only two new republics were established in Europe: the French in 1870 and the Portuguese in 1910 – both long-established nation-states.

Nor were any of the new states the ethnically homogeneous and inclusive nation-states of Mazzinian fantasy. Belgium was a linguistic hodge-podge; there were Rumanians aplenty outside Rumania; hardly any Italians spoke or felt themselves to be Italian (least of all in the south, which became a Piedmontese colony); nearly 10 million Germans did not live within the borders of the Reich (though sundry Poles and Danes did), which in any case was a federation, not a unitary nation-state. Moreover, for every state-building project that succeeded, there was one that failed. The Irish did not even manage to win back their parliament ('Home Rule'), though they were on the verge of doing so when war broke out. The Poles' heroic aspirations continued to be squashed by Russia and Prussia; partitioned four times (in 1772, 1793, 1795 and 1815), Poland made two abortive bids for independence in 1830 and 1863, only to be smashed by the Tsar's army. Self-government was a distant dream for the Croats, Rumanians and Germans who had to endure the uncompromising chauvinism of Magyar rule in Hungary. Other minorities were even more firmly under Russian control: Finns, Estonians, Latvians, Lithuanians, Ukrainians and others. A new state was made only to be unmade on the other side of the Atlantic; the Southern Confederacy failed to win its independence from the United States of America. If Bismarck won the German 'Civil War', then Jefferson Davis lost the South's 'War of Unification'.

There were also ethnic minorities who did not much want national independence before 1914, though some would later embrace it. The Czechs and Slovaks in Austria-Hungary, for example; but also the Jews there, with the exception of the few Zionists; and (in another multinational kingdom) the Scots, the majority of whom derived obvious material benefits from the Union and the Empire and who struck even the Czechs as woefully lacking in nationalist sentiment. At a reception after a football match between Slavie and Aberdeen (memorably described by Jaroslav Hašek), the Czech hosts attempt a cultural exchange, regaling their Scottish guests with 'the awakening of the Czech people', introducing them to such national heroes as Hus, Havlícek and Saint John Nepomuk, and singing the Czech anthem. The Scots, however, play not for love of country but for money (on £2 sterling a day), assume Havlícek is a former Slavie player and belt out 'a salty song about a pretty sutler lass'.

Finally, we should also remember the persistence of anomalous states and statelets that defied the first principles of nationalism: Switzerland, a multilingual confederation, or Luxembourg, a tiny but independent duchy enjoying the same international status as Belgium. There was no irresistible force called nationalism, insisting that Bosnia-Hercegovina could not remain as it was: a religiously heterogeneous province, formerly of the Ottoman Empire, then, after the Congress of Berlin's decision in 1878, occupied and administered by Austria-Hungary, and in 1908 formally incorporated (as a crown land under the control of the 'common' Austro-Hungarian Finance Ministry) into the Habsburg monarchy.

The Austrians piled soldiers and bureaucrats into Bosnia, stamped out banditry, built 200 primary schools, 1,000 kilometres of railways and 2,000 kilometres of roads, and tried vainly to improve agriculture (though when a good quality boar was sent to a village for breeding purposes, it was turned into the Christmas roast). In 1910 they established a Bosnian parliament. They even tried – vainly – to persuade the three different religious communities to think of themselves collectively as *Bošnjaci*. It was no use. The only thing Orthodox, Catholic and Muslim could agree on was that they did not care for Austrian rule; indeed, there were members of each of the religious communities in Mlada Bosna (Young Bosnia), a student terrorist group. The more the Austrians clamped down, the more determined the young terrorists became. When the Archduke Francis Ferdinand and his wife Sophie, Duchess of Hohenberg, decided to visit Sarajevo on 28 June (not only the national festival of Vidovdan, but also the anniversary of the Battle of Kosovo), members of Mlada Bosna resolved to kill them. At the second attempt, and thanks to the most famous wrong-turning in history, one of them, a consumptive Serbian student named Gavrilo Princip, succeeded. The Serbian government did not plan the assassination, though Princip and his associates had undoubtedly received assistance from the pan-Serb society the Black Hand, among the founders of which was the head of Serbian Military Intelligence, Colonel Dragutin Dimitrijevic. His superiors knew well that their chances of adding Bosnia-Hercegovina to their kingdom would not be improved by a war with the militarily superior Austria-Hungary. On the other hand, they also knew that a general European war might help them. As a Serb journalist told the British minister in Belgrade as early as 1898 (on the eve of the first Hague Peace Conference):

The idea of disarmament does not please our people in any way. The Servian race is split up under seven or eight different foreign governments, and we cannot be satisfied so long as this state of things lasts. We live in the hope of getting something for ourselves out of the general conflagration, whenever it takes place.

This was Serbian foreign policy: a kind of national-ist version of Lenin's dictum 'the worse, the better'. 'Ah yes,' said the Serbian Foreign Minister, 'if the disintegration of Austria-Hungary could take place at the same time as the liquidation of Turkey, the solution would be greatly simplified.' For this to happen, however, an Austrian action had to precipi-tate, at the very least, a Russian reaction.

Between 1878 and 1908, however, Balkan instability had not had serious ramifications. Since 1897 Austria and Russia had agreed not to disagree about the region. Indeed, the Austrian Foreign Minister Count Lexa von Aehrenthal consulted his Russian counterpart Alexander Izvolsky before proceeding to annex Bosnia. To be sure, there was a whiff of smoke in 1908–9 when Izvolsky, discovering belatedly that the concession on the Straits he had expected in return was not in Austria's gift, demanded that the annexation be approved by an inter-national conference. Germany, for so long the onlooker in Balkan quarrels, now strongly supported Vienna (the first time this had happened since the brief experiment of Chancellor Caprivi's 'new course' in the first years of William II's reign). Helmuth von Moltke, the Chief of the German General Staff, assured his Austrian counterpart Conrad: 'The moment Russia mobilizes, Germany will also mobilize, and will unquestionably mobilize her whole army.' Yet the immediate effect of German intervention was to reduce rather than increase the risk of war; the Russians were far from ready for another war so soon after their humiliation by Japan (in 1904–5), and backed down when it became clear that neither France nor Britain was sympathetic. Something similar happened in 1912, following the First Balkan War in which Serbia and Bulgaria, assisted by Montenegro and Greece, drove the Turks out of Kosovo, Macedonia and the Sandžak of Novi Pazar (left in Ottoman hands by the Congress of Berlin). Although the French made it clear that 'if Russia goes to war, France will also' and the Germans promised the Austrians 'unconditional . . . support', the truth was that neither St Petersburg nor Vienna wanted war. When Aehrenthal's successor Count Berchtold stated his terms – an independent Albania (a surprise to the Albanians) and a ban on the Serbs establishing a port on the Adriatic – the Russian Foreign Minister Sergei Sazonov assured the Serbs that they would get no Russian support if they insisted on the latter. (It should be noted that the Russians were bound by no treaty to assist Serbia in a war.) True, the Russians had upped the ante in the arms race by retaining the conscripts who would normally have completed their military service at the end of the year, but this was something of a reflex action. Their real worry was that the Bulgarians – over whom they had long since lost control – might gazump them by getting all the way to Constantinople. 'I think', the German Chancellor told Bethmann Berchtold in February 1913, 'it would be a mistake of immeasurable consequence if we attempt a solution by force . . . at a moment when there is even the remotest possibility of entering this conflict under conditions more favourable to ourselves.' When Bulgaria tried to wrest Macedonia from Serbia (and Salonika from Greece) by going to war in June 1913 – only to lose badly – Bethmann expressed the hope that 'Vienna would not let its peace be disturbed by the *cauchemar* of a Greater Serbia'. The most that Berchtold was prepared to do was to chase the Serbs out of Albanian territory.

What made the difference in 1914? Partly, the direct German interest in Turkey, signalled by the German military mission to Constantinople led by General Liman von Sanders; that scared the Russians, dependent as their finances were on grain exports through the Black Sea Straits, weakened as their own Black Sea fleet was, frail as Turkey looked after the Balkan wars. Indeed, this was one of the arguments for the Franco-Russian railway agreement of January 1914 and the arms programme approved by the Duma six months later. Partly, things were changed by the removal of Francis Ferdinand himself, who had been restraining the recklessly bellicose Conrad. But principally it was the German decision to support, indeed to egg on, an Austrian military strike against Serbia in order to end the threat posed by the 'Piedmont of the South Slavs' – in the Emperor Francis Joseph's words, to 'eliminate . . . Serbia as a political factor in the Balkans'. Both the Kaiser and Bethmann gave Count Szögyéni-Marich, the Habsburg ambassador, and Count Hoyos, whom Berchtold sent specially, a clear assurance: 'Even if it should come to a war between Austria and Russia . . . Germany would stand by our side.' The puzzle for the historian has always been to explain why the government in Berlin persisted with this venture in the face of ample evidence that it would indeed lead to a European war.

The Gamblers

It is true that during July the German decision-makers repeatedly expressed the hope that the conflict would be localized; in other words that Austria would be able to vanquish Serbia without Russian intervention. However, it is hard to reconcile such aspirations with the frequent allusions elsewhere to the likelihood of a more general conflagration. In February 1913, for example, Bethmann had rejected the idea of a preventive war against Serbia because 'Russian intervention . . . would result in a war-like conflict of the Triple Alliance . . . against the Triple Entente, and Germany would have to bear the full brunt of the French and British attack'. It is striking that when the Kaiser mentioned a preventive war to the banker Max Warburg, the latter clearly assumed he meant a war against Russia, France and Britain – despite his own involvement in attempts to seek a rapprochement with Britain on colonial issues. The Germans had good reason to fear that an Austrian move against Serbia would, if supported by Germany, lead to a full-scale European war. Sazonov made it clear from the moment the Austrian ultimatum to Serbia was published that Russia would react; while on 25 and 29 July 1914 the British Foreign Secretary Sir Edward Grey had restated the British position of December 1912: Should 'the position of France as a power' be threatened, England would not stand aside. Given these indications that the war would not be localized, there were ample opportunities for Berlin to back down. Yet the initial British peace-keeping initiatives were given only the most insincere support by Germany. The Germans pressed on, urging the Austrians to make haste, and after 26 July openly rejecting diplomatic alternatives. Only at the eleventh hour did they begin to lose their nerve: the Kaiser first, on 28 July, and then Bethmann who, after hearing of Grey's warning of the 29th to the German ambassador Prince Lichnowsky, frantically sought to persuade the Austrians to apply the brakes. Berchtold tried to respond, but it was the German military which ultimately secured, by a combination of persuasion and defiance, the mobilization orders, ultimata and declarations of war that unleashed the conflict.

It has, of course, been argued that the Russian decision to mobilize, partially or fully, played its part in unleashing the conflict. However, the Russian argument that their mobilization was not the same as the German and did not mean war was privately accepted by Moltke and Bethmann. By 27 July it is clear that the Germans' principal concern was, as Müller put it, 'to put Russia in the wrong and then not to shy away from war' – in other words, to portray the fact of Russian mobilization as evidence of an attack on Germany. German military intelligence pulled off the war's first espionage success in delivering evidence of Russian mobilization. Indications that the 'period preparatory to war' had been proclaimed on the night of 25 July reached Berlin on the morning of Monday the 27th, though Bethmann had already quoted 'unconfirmed news' of this 'from [a] reliable source' in his dispatch to Lichnowsky the previous afternoon. Early reports that general mobilization had been ordered by the Tsar arrived in Berlin on the evening of 30 July, though it was not until the following morning that Moltke was convinced, and even then he insisted on one of the red Russian mobilization posters being obtained and read aloud over the telephone. An hour later, the Germans proclaimed their 'imminent danger of war'.

Why did the Germans act as they did? The best answer that can be offered by the diplomatic historian relates to the structure of European alliances, which had clearly tilted against Berlin since the turn of the century. Russia, France and England had all been able to find issues on which they could agree, but Germany had repeatedly failed (or chosen not) to secure comparable 'ententes'. Even such allies as they did have seemed less than reliable: declining Austria, unreliable Italy. It can therefore be argued that the Germans saw a confrontation over the Balkans as a means of preserving their own fragile alliance with Austria, possibly also creating an anti-Russian Balkan alliance and perhaps even splitting the Triple Entente. Such calculations were by no means unrealistic. As events proved, there was good reason to doubt the Triple Alliance's dependability, and the Triple Entente was indeed fragile, especially where England was concerned. Even before the July crisis began, Colonel Edward House, Woodrow Wilson's envoy to Europe, discerned that 'what Germany really wants is for England to detach herself from the Triple Entente'. Even French support for Russia, although expressed enthusiastically by the ambassador Maurice Paléologue, seemed to waver on 30 July and 1 August. It is therefore possible that, despite being well aware of the implications of war with respect to Belgium, Bethmann and the German Foreign Minister Gottlieb von Jagow discerned just enough evidence of dissension within the Triple Entente for the Germans to continue to hope for British neutrality. They knew the risks with respect to Belgium. On 28 April 1913 Jagow himself had refused to provide the Reichstag Budget Committee with a guarantee of Belgian neutrality, since it would give the French 'a pointer as to where to expect us' – one of those revealing denials that were his peculiar forte. But he and Bethmann chose to gamble for the prize of a diplomatic victory.

Yet none of this satisfactorily explains why the German generals were so determined to go to war and continue fighting *even if the Triple Entente held*; and this is the critical point since it was they who pressed for mobilization after the diplomatic gamble had failed. At this point the military historian offers an explanation, based on the German General Staff's pessimistic calculations about the relative present and future strengths of the European armies, on which depended their argument for a pre-emptive or preventive war. This was a case that had repeatedly been rejected in the past. But in the summer of 1914 it was once again on the *Tagesordnung* as Moltke waged a campaign to convince the Kaiser, the civilian authorities and the Austrians that, as a result of new armaments programmes in France and Russia, Germany would be at their mercy within a few years. 'Prospects could never come better for us,' argued the Deputy Chief of the General Staff, Georg Count Waldersee, on 3 July, referring to Russia's unpreparedness, a view repeated by the Kaiser three days later: 'Russia is at the present moment militarily and financially totally unprepared for war.' On 6–7 July, Bethmann's confidant Kurt Riezler recorded that military intelligence gave 'a shattering picture': 'After the completion of their [the Russians'] strategic railroads in Poland our position will be untenable . . . The Entente knows that we are completely paralysed.' Szögyéni reported the German argument to Berchtold on 12 July: 'Should the Tsar's Empire resolve for war, it would not be so ready from a military point of view and not by any means so strong as it will be in a few years' time.' Jagow duly relayed the argument to Lichnowsky in London on July 18: 'Russia is not yet ready to strike at present . . . [but] according to all competent observation, [she] will be prepared to fight in a few years. Then she will crush us by the number of soldiers; then she will have built her Baltic Sea Fleet and her strategic railroads.' On July 25 the journalist Theodor Wolff was told by Jagow that although 'neither Russia nor France wanted war . . . The Russians . . . were not ready with their armaments, they would not strike; in two years' time, if we let matters slide, the danger would be much greater than at present.' 'War will come soon anyway,' Jagow assured Wolff, and the situation now was 'very favourable'. When Moltke returned to Berlin the next day, therefore, the ground had already been well prepared for his argument: 'We shall never again strike as well as we do now, with France's and Russia's expansion of their armies incomplete.' Bethmann had been persuaded at last: 'If war must break out, better now than in one or two years' time when the Entente will be stronger.' Whenever he showed signs of wavering in the subsequent days, Moltke stiffened his resolve with a reminder: 'The military situation is becoming from day to day more unfavourable for us and can, if our prospective opponents prepare themselves further unmolested, lead to fateful consequences for us.' Thus what began as an argument in favour of war this year rather than in two years became an argument for mobilization today rather than tomorrow.

That the Germans were thinking along these lines was no secret. Grey himself twice commented in July 1914 on the logic, from a German point of view, of a pre-emptive strike against Russia and France, before the military balance deteriorated any further:

The truth is that whereas formerly the German government had aggressive intentions . . . they are now genuinely alarmed at the military preparations in Russia, the prospective increase in her military forces and particularly at the intended construction, at the insistence of the French government and with French money, of strategic railways to converge on the German frontier . . . Germany was not afraid, because she believed her army to be invulnerable, but she was afraid that in a few years hence she might be afraid . . . Germany was afraid of the future.

His only mistake was to think that this would keep the German government 'in a peaceful mood'. On 30 July the German diplomat Count Kanitz told the American ambassador that 'G[ermany] should go to war when they are prepared and not wait until Russia has completed her plan to have a peace footing of 2,400,000 men'. Colonel House reported to President

Wilson on 1 August that Germany knew 'that her best chance is to strike quickly and hard'; she might 'precipitate action as a means of safety'.

The Kaiser's verdict on 30 July was, of course, divorced from reality: 'England, Russia and France have agreed among themselves . . . to take the Austro-Serbian conflict for an excuse for waging a war of extermination against us . . . The famous encirclement of Germany has finally become a complete fact . . . We squirm isolated in the net.' But he was not the only person to perceive the German position as vulnerable. House's famous remark about 'jingoism run mad' in his letter to Wilson of 29 May should be seen in context:

The situation is extraordinary. It is jingoism run stark mad. Unless someone acting for you can bring about a different understanding, there is some day to be an awful cataclysm. No one in Europe can do it. There is too much hatred, too many jealousies. Whenever England consents, France and Russia will close in on Germany and Austria.

House was later dismissive of British claims to be 'fighting for Belgium'. Britain had sided with France and Russia 'primarily . . . because Germany insisted upon having a dominant army and a dominant navy, something Great Britain could not tolerate in safety to herself'. And he was no Germanophile: after visiting Berlin he remarked that he had 'never seen the war spirit so nurtured and so glorified as it is there . . . Their one thought is to advance industrially and to glorify war.' House was also an early proponent of the theory that Germany had gone to war partly in order that the 'group of militarists and financiers' who governed her could 'conserve their selfish interests'. But his analysis left room for the possibility that German security had indeed been threatened.

There is thus no need to posit, as Fritz Fischer did, pre-existing German war plans to create spheres of influence in Central Europe and Africa, to destroy France as a power and to carve up Russia's Western Empire. The evidence points far more persuasively to a military 'first strike', designed to pre-empt a deterioration in Germany's military position – though this is by no means incompatible with the idea that the outcome of such a strike, if successful, would have been German hegemony in Europe. The only real question is whether or not this strategy deserves the apologetic name of 'preventive war'. It is to condescend to the German decision-makers to caricature them as irrational duellists, going to war 'in a fit of anger', for the sake of an antiquated sense of honour. The Germans did not care about losing 'face'; they cared about losing the arms race.

That said, the extent of German malice aforethought must not be exaggerated. For men who were planning a war, the senior members of the Great General Staff were uncannily relaxed in July 1914. At the time the Kaiser issued his famous 'blank cheque' to the Austrians, Moltke, Waldersee, Lieutenant Colonel Wilhelm Groener, chief of the Railway Section, and Major Nicolai, the head of key intelligence agency 'Section IIIb', were all on holiday (in separate resorts, it should be said). Grand Admiral Tirpitz and Admiral Pohl were too. It was only on 16 July that Nicolai's stand-in, Captain Kurt Neuhof, was advised to step up surveillance of Russian military activity. Waldersee returned from Mecklenburg on 23 July, but Nicolai himself was not back at his desk for another two days. Even then, his orders to the so-called 'tension travellers' (*Spannungsreisende*) – i.e. German spies in Russia and France – were merely to find out 'whether war preparations are taking place in France and Russia'.

Smashing the Telephone

With hindsight, the biggest question of 1914 – the one that would decide the war – was what Britain would do. At the time, however, it seemed unimportant to many of the key decision-makers on the continent. Though Bethmann sometimes dreamt of British neutrality, the German generals were indifferent; they doubted that Britain's small army could influence the outcome of a war. Nor did the French generals care much. The Chief of the French General Staff, Joseph-Jacques-Césaire Joffre, was bullish enough to believe that he could win the war in the West without assistance.

When, in the wake of the Sarajevo assassinations, it became clear in London that the Austrian government intended demanding 'some compensation in the sense of some humiliation for Serbia', Grey's first reaction was to worry about how Russia might react. Seeing the possibility of a confrontation between Austria and Russia, he sought to exert indirect pressure *via* Berlin to temper any Austrian reprisals; he hoped to repeat the success of his Balkan diplomacy the previous year. The Russian ambassador in Vienna made it clear as early as 8 July that 'Russia would be compelled to take up arms in defence of Serbia' if Austria 'rushed into war'; Grey's belief that a distinction could be drawn between cessions of territory by Serbia and some less serious form of reprisal was never really shared in St Petersburg. (Revealingly, Grey warned Lichnowsky that 'in view of the present unpopularity of England in Russia' he would 'have to be careful of Russian feelings'.) At first Grey urged Austria and Russia to 'discuss things together' in the hope that terms could be devised for the Serbs that both sides would find acceptable, but this was dismissed by the French president, Raymond Poincaré, who happened to be visiting St Petersburg. Doubting his ability to exercise a moderating influence over Russia, and suspecting that the German government might actually be 'egging on' the Austrians (a suspicion confirmed by the terms of their ultimatum to Serbia), Grey changed tack, warning Lichnowsky that Russia would stand by Serbia and suggesting mediation between Austria and Russia by the four other powers.

From the outset Grey was extremely reluctant to give any indication of how Britain might respond to an escalation of the conflict. He knew that if Austria pressed extreme demands on Belgrade with German backing, and Russia mobilized in defence of Serbia, then France might well become involved – such was the nature of the Franco-Russian alliance and German military strategy, so far as it was known in London. Part of Grey's strategy in trying to turn the ententes with France and Russia into quasi-alliances had been to deter Germany from risking war. However, he now feared that too strong a signal of support for France and Russia – such as the hawkish Sir Eyre Crowe and Sir Arthur Nicolson urged – might encourage the Russians to do just that. Grey found himself in a cleft stick: how to deter Austria and Germany without encouraging France and Russia. This explains his characteristically convoluted statement to Lichnowsky on 24 July that:

there was no alliance . . . committing us to . . . France and Russia . . . On the other hand . . . the British government belonged to one group of powers, but did not do so in order to make difficulties greater between the two European groups; on the contrary, we wished to prevent any questions that arose from throwing the groups . . . into opposition . . . We should never pursue an aggressive policy, and if there was a European war, and we took part in it, it would not be on the aggressive side, for public opinion was against that.

Lichnowsky interpreted this, as Grey doubtless intended, as a warning that 'in case France should be drawn in, England would [not] dare to remain disinterested', a point he repeated with growing anxiety as the crisis intensified. But Bethmann and Jagow evidently concluded that a show of German support for four-power mediation would suffice to satisfy Grey. The King took a similarly ambiguous line with the Kaiser's brother when they met on 26 July:

I don't know what we shall do, we have no quarrel with anyone and I hope we shall remain neutral. But if Germany declared war on Russia and France joins Russia, then I am afraid we shall be dragged into it. But you can be sure that I and my government will do all we can to prevent a European war.

Prince Heinrich concluded that England would remain neutral 'at the beginning', though he doubted 'whether she will be able to do so in the long run . . . on account of her relations with France'. However, neutrality in the short run might be all the German government needed if the army could establish a strong enough military position on the continent. In short, British policy was so garbled that it could be interpreted more or less according to taste. By Sunday 26 July the French thought they could count on Britain, while the Germans felt 'sure' of English neutrality. As Jagow put it to Paul Cambon: 'You have your information. We have ours'; unfortunately, the source was identical in each case. The German government continued undeterred, feigning interest in Grey's proposals for mediation, which it had no intention of pursuing.

To be fair to Grey, his tactic of studied ambiguity very nearly paid off. So exposed did the Serbian government feel itself to be, that – despite Grey's dismay at Vienna's 'formidable' terms – it all but accepted the Austrian ultimatum, seeking only the most limited modifications to it. Moreover, to the dismay of both Bethmann and Moltke, who had been urging the Austrians not to take Grey's mediation proposal seriously, the Kaiser hailed the Serbian reply as a diplomatic triumph. In the belief that *'every cause for war* [now] falls to the ground', he urged Vienna simply to 'Halt in Belgrade', in other words to occupy the Serbian capital temporarily, much as Prussia had occupied Northern France in 1870, 'as a guaranty for the enforcement and carrying out of the promises'. This compounded the confusion that Jagow had created by stating that Germany would *not* act if Russia mobilized only in the south (that is, against Austria but not Germany). At the same time Sazonov unexpectedly changed his mind about the possibility of bilateral talks between Austria and Russia, an idea Grey immediately returned to when it became clear that the German government did not really favour his scheme for a four-power conference. As Nicolson commented huffily, 'One does not really know where one is with Mr Sazonov.' (Nor did one know where one was with the Germans; Jagow now argued that a four-power conference would 'amount to a court of arbitration', putting Austria and Serbia on an equal footing, while at the same time Bethmann deliberately omitted to mention Sazonov's proposal for bilateral talks to Lichnowsky on the ground that the ambassador was 'informing Sir Edward [Grey] of everything'.) For a moment, it seemed that the continental war might be averted. To be sure, Sazonov had no intention of accepting the occupation of Belgrade by Austria, which would have represented in his eyes a serious reverse for Russian influence in the Balkans. But he declared himself willing to halt mobilization 'if Austria . . . declares itself ready to eliminate from its ultimatum those points which infringe on Serbia's sovereign rights'. An increasingly desperate Bethmann seized on this as a basis for negotiation and the Austrian government actually accepted Sazonov's offer of talks on 30 July.

Unfortunately, however, military logic had now begun to supersede diplomatic calculation. Even before the Austrian bombardment of Belgrade began, Sazonov and his military colleagues issued orders for partial mobilization, which they then desperately tried to turn into full mobilization on being warned that Germany in fact intended to mobilize even in the case of Russian partial mobilization. The Russians in fact began mobilizing in the southern districts of Odessa, Kiev, Moscow and Kazan on 29 July – a decision which the Tsar later said had been taken four days before – assuring the German ambassador Count Pourtalès that this was 'far from meaning war'. But on being told by Pourtalès that Germany would none the less 'find herself compelled to mobilise, in which case she would immediately proceed to the offensive', the Russians concluded that a partial mobilization would be inadequate, and might even jeopardize full mobilization. There followed a hysterical series of meetings and telephone conversations as Sazonov and his colleagues tried to persuade the vacillating Tsar to agree to full mobilization. He finally did so at 2 p.m. on 30 July and mobilization began the next day. (As in Berlin, the much-vaunted power of the monarch proved to be illusory at the moment of decision.) This was precisely the pretext the Germans wanted to launch their own mobilization against not only Russia but also France. The idea of Austro-Russian talks was forgotten in a bizarre 'reverse race', in which, for the sake of domestic opinion, Germany tried to get Russia to mobilize first. Continental war was now surely unavoidable. Even when Bethmann, grasping at last that Britain might intervene immediately in response to an attack on France, sought to force the Austrians to the negotiating table, the soldiers refused to suspend their military operations. Royal appeals to St Petersburg to halt mobilization were equally futile, as the Chief of the Russian

General Staff, General Nikolai Yanushkevich, had resolved (as he told Sazonov) to 'smash my telephone and generally adopt measures which will prevent anyone [i.e. the Tsar] from finding me for the purpose of giving contrary orders which would again stop our mobilization'. And if Russia continued to mobilize, the Germans insisted they had no option but to do the same. That meant the invasion of Belgium and France. In short, 'war by timetable' commenced the moment Russia decided on full mobilization – that is, war by timetable between the four continental powers (as well, of course, as Serbia and Belgium). What still nevertheless remained avoidable was Britain's involvement (and, for that matter, the involvement of Turkey and Italy).

Why Britain Fought

Not surprisingly, it was at this point that the French and Russian governments began seriously pressing Grey to make Britain's position clear. The French argued that if Grey were to 'announce that in the event of a conflict between Germany and France ... England would come to the aid of France, there would be no war'. But Grey, who had been trying for some days to intimate this to Lichnowsky, knew that he alone could not make such a commitment to France. True, he already had the hawks at the Foreign Office behind him arguing that a 'moral bond' had been 'forged' by the Entente (Crowe), and that therefore 'We should at once give orders for the mobilisation of the army' (Nicolson). But, as had repeatedly been made clear since 1911, he could not act without the support of his Cabinet colleagues and his party – to say nothing of that nebulous and frequently invoked entity 'public opinion'. And it was far from clear that he could rely on any of these to back an explicit military commitment to France. It was therefore decided simply to decide nothing, 'for [as Herbert Samuel put it] if both sides do not know what we shall do, both will be the less willing to run risks'. The most Grey could do was once again to tell Lichnowsky *privately* – 'to spare himself later the reproach of bad faith' – that 'if [Germany] and France should be involved, then . . . the British government would . . . find itself forced to make up its mind quickly. In that event, it would not be practicable to stand aside and wait for any length of time.' That this impressed Bethmann where Grey's previous statements had not can be explained by the fact that, for the first time, Grey implied that any British action in defence of France would be swift. An equally deep impression was made in London by Bethmann's bid for British neutrality – which he made just before he heard Grey's warning to Lichnowsky – principally because it made Germany's intention to attack France so blatantly obvious. But although it was sharply rebuffed, even this did not prompt a commitment to intervene, and the Admiralty's limited naval preparations of 28–29

July certainly did not have the same significance as the continental armies' mobilization orders. On the contrary: having issued his private warning, Grey took a markedly *softer* official line with Germany, in a last bid to revive the idea of four-power mediation. Indeed, on the morning of 31 July Grey went so far as to say to Lichnowsky:

If Germany could get any reasonable proposal put forward which made it clear that Germany and Austria were still striving to preserve European peace, and that Russia and France would be unreasonable if they rejected it, I would support it . . . and go the length of saying that if Russia and France would not accept it, His Majesty's Government would have nothing more to do with the consequences.

The 'reasonable proposal' Grey had in mind was that 'Germany would agree not to attack France if France remained neutral [or kept her troops on her own territory] in the event of a war between Russia and Germany'. Even the pessimistic Lichnowsky began to think on hearing this that 'in a possible war, England might adopt a waiting attitude'. Reactions in Paris were correspondingly bleak. On the evening of 1 August Grey told Jules Cambon baldly:

If France could not take advantage of this position [i.e. proposal], it was because she was bound by an alliance to which we were not parties, and of which we did not know the terms . . . France must take her own decision at this moment without reckoning on an assistance that we were not now in a position to promise . . . We could not propose to Parliament at this moment to send an expeditionary military force to the Continent . . . unless our interests and obligations were deeply and desperately involved.

A private warning to Lichnowsky was not, as Grey explained to Cambon, 'the same thing as . . . an engagement to France'. Grey was not even prepared to give the Belgian ambassador a guarantee that 'if Germany violates the neutrality of Belgium, we would certainly assist Belgium' – although later the government would make much of its legal obliga- tion to do so.

Grey's conduct in these crucial days was circum- scribed by domestic political considerations. As we have seen, there was a substantial body of Liberal politicians and journalists who strongly opposed such a commit- ment. On 30 July twenty-two Liberal members of the backbench Foreign Affairs Committee intimated through Arthur Ponsonby that 'any decision in favour of participation in a European war would meet not only with the strongest disapproval but with the actual withdrawal of support from the Government'. The Prime Minister, Herbert Asquith, estimated that around three-quarters of his parliamentary party were for 'absolute non-interference at any price'. The Cabinet roughly reflected this, with the proponents of the continental commitment still in a decided minority. The nineteen men who met on 31 July were divided into three unequal groups: those who, in common with the bulk of the party, favoured an immediate declaration of neutrality (including Viscount Morley, Sir John Simon, John Burns, Earl Beauchamp and Charles Hobhouse), those who were in favour of intervention (only Grey and the bellicose First Lord of the Admiralty, Winston Churchill) and those who had not made up their minds (notably Reginald McKenna, Viscount Haldane, Herbert Samuel, Lewis Harcourt, the Quaker Joseph Pease and the Marquess of Crewe, but probably also the Chancellor of the Exchequer, David Lloyd George – as well, of course, as Asquith himself). Morley argued forcefully against intervention on the side of Russia, and it seemed clear that the majority was inclining to his view. However, Grey's threat to resign if 'an out-and-out uncompromising policy of non-intervention' were adopted sufficed to maintain the stalemate. The Cabinet agreed that 'British opinion would not now enable us to support France . . . we could say nothing to commit ourselves'.

Nor was the deadlock really broken when, on the night of 1 August, while Grey played billiards at Brooks's, Churchill was able to persuade Asquith to let him mobilize the navy on the news of the German declaration of war on Russia. This merely prompted Morley and Simon to threaten resignation at the next morning's meeting and the majority once again to close ranks against Grey's repeated pleas for an un-ambiguous declaration of commitment. The most that could be agreed in the first session of that crucial Sunday was that 'if the German fleet comes into the Channel or through the North Sea to undertake hostile operations against the French coasts or shipping, the British fleet will give all the protection in its power'. Even this – which was far from being a declaration of war, given that such German naval action was quite unlikely – was too much for Burns, the President of the Board of Trade, who resigned. As Samuel noted, 'Had the matter come to an issue, Asquith would have stood by Grey . . . and three others would have remained. I think the rest of us would have resigned.' At lunch at Beauchamp's that day, seven ministers, among them Lloyd George, expressed reservations about even the limited naval measures. Morley felt with hindsight that if Lloyd George had given a lead to the waverers, 'the Cabinet would undoubtedly have perished that evening'; but Harcourt's appeal to Lloyd George to 'speak for us' was in vain. Had they realized that Grey had already surreptitiously 'dropped' his proposal to Lichnowsky for French neutrality in a Russo-German war, and that Lichnowsky had been reduced to tears at Asquith's breakfast table that morning, they might have acted on those reservations. As it was, Morley, Simon and Beauchamp now joined Burns in offering their resignations, following the commitment to Belgium which Grey had only been able to secure that evening by himself threatening to resign. A junior minister, Charles Trevelyan, also handed in his notice.

So why did the government not fall? The immediate answer is, as Asquith recorded in his diary, that Lloyd George, Samuel and Pease appealed to the resigners 'not to go, or at least to delay it' whereupon 'they agreed to say nothing today and sit in their accustomed places in the House'. But why did only Morley, Burns and Trevelyan in the end quit? The traditional answer can be expressed in a single word: Belgium.

Certainly, it had long been recognized in the Foreign Office that the decision to intervene on behalf of France 'would be more easily arrived at if German aggressiveness . . . entailed a violation of the neutrality of Belgium'. And Lloyd George and others later cited the violation of Belgian neutrality as the single most important reason for swinging them – and 'public opinion' – in favour of war. At first sight, the point seems irrefutable. Britain's 'solemn international obligation' to uphold Belgian neutrality in the name of law and honour, and 'to vindicate the principle . . . that small nations are not to be crushed', provided the two central themes of Asquith's 'What are we fighting for?' speech to the Commons on 6 August 1914. It was also the keynote of Lloyd George's successful Welsh recruitment drive.

Nevertheless there are reasons for scepticism. As we have seen, the Foreign Office view in 1905 had been that the 1839 treaty did not bind Britain to uphold Belgium's neutrality 'in any circumstances and at whatever risk'. When the issue had come up in 1912, none other than Lloyd George had expressed the concern that, in the event of war, the preservation of Belgian neutrality would undermine the British blockade strategy. Significantly, when the issue was raised in Cabinet on 29 July, it was decided to base any response to a German invasion of Belgium on 'policy' rather than 'legal obligation'. The government's line was therefore to warn the Germans obliquely by stating that a violation of Belgium might cause British public opinion to 'veer round'. Thus Grey was able to respond to German prevarication on the subject with a unanimous Cabinet warning that 'if there were a violation of Belgian neutrality . . . it would be extremely hard to restrain public feeling'. But that did not commit the government itself. This is not so surprising, as a number of ministers were in fact rather keen to welch on the Belgian guarantee.

Lloyd George was one of those who, as Lord Beaverbrook later recalled, tried to argue that the Germans would 'pass only through the furthest southern corner' and that this would imply 'a small infraction of neutrality. "You see", he would say [pointing to a map], "it is only a little bit, and the Germans will pay for any damage they do."' It was widely (though wrongly) expected, in any case, that the Belgians would not call for British assistance, but would simply issue a formal protest in the event of a German passage through the Ardennes. The German bid for British neutrality on 29 July had very clearly implied an incursion into Belgium; but even on the morning of 2 August, after Jagow had refused to guarantee Belgian neutrality, Lloyd George, Harcourt, Beauchamp, Simon, and Pease agreed that they could contemplate war only in the event of 'the invasion *wholesale* of Belgium'. Sir Walter Runciman and Charles Trevelyan took the same view. Hence the careful wording of the Cabinet's resolution that evening, communicated by Crewe to the King, that 'a *substantial* violation of the neutrality of [Belgium] would place us in the situation contemplated as possible by Mr Gladstone in 1870, when interference was held to compel us to take action'.

The news of the German ultimatum to Belgium therefore came as something of a relief to Asquith when it reached him on the morning of 3 August. Moltke's demand for unimpeded passage through the *whole* of Belgium, the subsequent appeal of King Albert, indicating that Belgium intended to resist any infraction of her neutrality, and the German invasion the next day distinctly 'simplified matters', in Asquith's words, because it allowed both Simon and Beauchamp to withdraw their resignations. The last-minute attempts by Moltke and Lichnowsky to guarantee the post-war integrity of Belgium were therefore as futile as the Germans' cynical lies about a French advance into Belgium. When Bethmann lamented to Sir William Goschen that 'England should fall upon them for the sake of the neutrality of Belgium' – for '*un chiffon de papier*' – he was missing the point. By requiring a German advance through the whole of Belgium, the Schlieffen Plan helped save the Liberal government.

Yet it was not the German threat to Belgium which swung the Cabinet behind intervention so much as the German threat to *Britain* that Grey and the hawks at the Foreign Office had always insisted would arise if France fell. This can be inferred from Asquith's note to his mistress Venetia Stanley of 2 August in which he set down the six principles by which he was guided; only the sixth referred to Britain's 'obligations to Belgium to prevent her being utilized and absorbed by Germany'. The fourth and fifth were more important, stating as they did that, while Britain was under no obligation to assist France, 'It is against British interests that France should be wiped out as a Great Power,' and 'We cannot allow Germany to use the Channel as a hostile base.' Likewise, the main argument of Grey's famous speech to the Commons of 3 August – delivered before the news of the German ultimatum to Belgium – was that 'if France is beaten in a struggle of life and death . . . I do not believe that . . . we should be in a position to use our force decisively to . . . prevent the whole of the West of Europe opposite to us . . . falling under the domination of a single Power.' The strategic risks of non-intervention – isolation, friendlessness – outweighed the risks of intervention. As Grey put it in a private conversation the next day: 'It will not end with Belgium. Next will come Holland, and after Holland, Denmark . . .

England['s] . . . position would be gone if Germany were thus permitted to dominate Europe.' German policy, he told the Cabinet, was 'that of the great European aggressor, as bad as Napoleon'. That this argument also won over waverers like Harcourt seems clear. As Asquith explained on 5 August:

I have acted not from any obligation of Treaty or of honour, for neither existed . . . There were three overwhelming British interests which I could not abandon:

1. That the German fleet should not occupy, under our neutrality, the North Sea and English Channel.
2. That they should not seize and occupy the North-Western part of France opposite our shores.
3. That they should not violate the ultimate independence of Belgium and hereafter occupy Antwerp as a standing menace to us.

This had been Pitt's argument for fighting France – an argument rooted in the assumption that sea power was the alpha and omega of British security. (The first Zeppelin raid exposed its obsolescence.) Morley was thus not far wrong when he said that Belgium had furnished a 'plea . . . for intervention on behalf of France'. This was also the view of Frances Stevenson, Lloyd George's mistress, and Ramsay MacDonald, who dined with Lloyd George on the evening of 2 August.

There was, however, another and arguably even more important reason why Britain went to war at

11 p.m. on 4 August 1914. Throughout the days of 31 July–3 August one thing above all maintained Cabinet unity: the fear of letting in the Conservative and Unionist opposition. It must be remembered how bitter relations between the two major parties had become by 1914; after the battles over Lloyd George's budgets and the powers of the House of Lords, the Liberals' decision once again to try to enact Home Rule for Ireland had inflamed Unionist sentiment. Attempts to reach a compromise over the temporary exclusion of Northern Ireland had failed at the Buckingham Palace conference. With Ulster Protestants arming themselves to prevent the imposition of 'Rome Rule' – the Ulster Volunteer Force had 100,000 men and at least 37,000 rifles – the possibility of civil war was real and the attitude of leading Tories, to say nothing of senior army officers, was not unsympathetic to the Protestant cause. The sudden onset of the European diplomatic crisis served, as Asquith remarked, to pour oil on the stormy Irish waters (that was 'the one bright spot in this hateful war'); but at the same time it gave the Tories a new stick with which to beat the government. For it had long been obvious that the Conservative leadership viewed the German threat more seriously than most Liberal ministers. In 1912, for example, Balfour had published an article on Anglo-German relations in which he explicitly accused the German government of planning a war of aggression with the purpose of resurrecting the Holy Roman Empire on the continent and

extending her overseas empire. Britain, he wrote, had:

too bitter an experience of the ills which flow from the endeavour of any single state to dominate Europe; we are too surely convinced of the perils which such a policy, were it successful, would bring upon ourselves . . . to treat them as negligible.

As we have seen, Grey was regarded by the Tories as a 'sound man', carrying on their own policies as best he could against the opposition of very unsound colleagues. But since 1911 the Foreign Secretary had been on the defensive, if not in retreat. Unionists like Frederick Oliver were appalled at the prospect of a crucial foreign policy decision being taken by 'a government which has so messed and misconceived our domestic situation'. Looking back on the crisis in December 1914, Austen Chamberlain expressed what was probably the dominant Conservative view of the Liberals' handling of the crisis:

There had been nothing beforehand in official speeches or official publications to make known to [our people] the danger that we ran to prepare them for the discharge of our responsibilities and the defence of our interests. Those who knew most were silent; those who undertook to instruct the mass of the public were ignorant, and our democracy with its decisive voice on the conduct of public affairs was left without guidance by those who could have

directed it properly, and was misled by those who consti-
tuted themselves its guides.

His brother Neville shared his dismay: 'It fairly makes
one gasp', he had exclaimed in August, 'to think that
we were within a hair's breadth of eternal disgrace.'

The cue for Tory action was provided by the knife-
edge Cabinet meetings of 2 August. That morning,
at the suggestion of a number of senior Tories, the
Unionist leader Bonar Law wrote to Asquith making
clear the Tory view that 'any hesitation in now
supporting France and Russia would be fatal to the
honour and future security of the United Kingdom'.
The 'united support' offered by Bonar Law 'in all
measures required by England's intervention in the
war' was nothing less than a veiled threat that
Conservatives would be willing to step into Liberal
shoes if the government could not agree on such
measures. After years of bellicose criticism from the
Tory press, this was the one thing calculated to harden
Asquith's resolve. Resignation, he told the Cabinet,
might seem the ordinary course for a government so
divided. But, he went on, 'the National situation is far
from ordinary, and I cannot persuade myself that the
other party is led by men, or contains men, capable
of dealing with it'. Samuel and Pease immediately
grasped the point, telling Burns: 'For the majority of
the Cabinet now to leave meant a ministry which was
a war one and that was the last thing he wanted.' 'The
alternative government', as Pease put it, 'must be one

much less anxious for peace than ourselves.' He said the same to Trevelyan three days later, by which time Simon and Runciman had taken up the refrain. Margot Asquith later remarked that it was 'lucky for this country that the Liberals were in power in 1914, as men might have been suspicious of acquiescing in such a terrible decision at the dictation of a Jingo Government'.

Probably unbeknown to the rest of the Cabinet, one of their own number was in fact poised to defect if the advocates of neutrality won the day. As early as 31 July Churchill secretly asked Bonar Law *via* F. E. Smith whether, in the event of up to eight resignations, 'the Opposition [would] be prepared to come to the rescue of the Government . . . by forming a Coalition to fill up the vacant offices'. Bonar Law declined Churchill's invitation to dine with him and Grey on 2 August, but his letter to the Cabinet had said enough. This was not the first time the idea of a coalition had been broached by a member of Asquith's government. None other than Lloyd George had flirted with the idea in 1910.

At first sight, the fact that the Conservatives were more eager than the Liberals for war might seem to strengthen the case for an inevitable British intervention; if Asquith had fallen, then Bonar Law would have gone to war just the same. But would it have been just the same? Let us suppose Lloyd George – defeated on his Finance Bill, beset by financial panic, assailed by pacifist editorials in the *Guardian* and the

British Weekly – had deserted Grey at the critical Cabinet meeting on 2 August and given leadership to the opponents of intervention. Grey would certainly have resigned; Churchill would have rushed off to join Bonar Law. Would Asquith have been able to hang on? Almost certainly not. But how quickly could a Conservative government have been formed? The last change of government had been a protracted affair: Balfour's administration had shown the first signs of disintegrating over tariff reform as early as 1903, had actually been defeated in the Commons on 20 July 1905, had lost the confidence of the Chamberlainites the following November and had finally resigned on 4 December. The general election which confirmed the strength of Liberal support in the country was not over until 7 February 1906. It is conceivable that matters would have moved more swiftly had Asquith been forced to resign in early August 1914. Certainly Churchill's plan for a coalition was designed to minimize delay. But would a declaration of war on Germany have been possible under such circumstances before a general election? Much would have depended on the King, who, like his cousins in Berlin and St Petersburg, had shown little enthusiasm for war once he looked over the edge of the abyss. It seems reasonable to assume that a change of government would have delayed the despatch of the British Expeditionary Force (BEF) by at least a week.

In any case, even with the government unchanged, the despatch of the BEF was not a foregone conclusion and did not go according to the plans which had been worked out in consultation with the French General Staff. This was because, as we have seen, a clear decision in favour of the continental commitment had never actually been made, so that all the old arguments against it immediately resurfaced when war broke out. The navalists insisted, as they had always insisted, that sea power alone could decide the war and until 5 August most ministers seemed to agree. Indeed, Sir Francis Bertie reported from Paris that the expeditionary force would not be needed; he was assured by General Edouard de Castelnau, Deputy Chief of the French General Staff, that 'the French, even if they suffer reverses, must win in the end, provided that England will aid by closing the sea approaches to Germany'. They also tended to favour keeping part or all of the army at home – not to fend off an invasion, which was not expected, but to preserve social peace (the economic consequences of the war were indeed already making themselves felt). At the 'rather motley' war council of generals and ministers called by Asquith on 5 August, confusion reigned and no decision was reached pending consultation with a representative of the French General Staff. The next day the Cabinet decided to send just four infantry divisions and the one available cavalry division to Amiens, whereas the Director of Military Operations, Sir Henry Wilson, had long before resolved to send all seven available divisions to Maubeuge to aid the

French. It was only six days later that Earl Kitchener, hastily recalled from Egypt and installed as Secretary of State for War, was persuaded to revert to Maubeuge, and not until 3 September that the Cabinet agreed to send the last remaining division to France.

Did it – as its proponents claimed and subsequent apologists have argued – make a decisive difference to the outcome of the war? Was Major A. H. Ollivant right to argue in his memorandum for Lloyd George of 1 August that 'the presence or absence of the British army will . . . very probably decide the fate of France'? In fact, the German advance would probably have failed to reach even without the BEF, such were the logistical shortcomings of Schlieffen's design, as modified by Moltke. Perhaps the French could there-fore have halted the German offensive unassisted, had they themselves not attempted to launch their own almost suicidal offensive rather than concentrating on defence. But they did not; and, even allowing for German errors, it seems likely that, despite the initial, desperate retreat from Mons and the failure of the feint at Ostend, the presence of British troops at Le Cateau on 26 August and at the Marne (6–9 September) *did* significantly reduce the chances of German victory. Unfortunately, what it could not do was to bring about a German defeat. After the fall of Antwerp and the first battle of Ypres (20 October– 22 November), a bloody stalemate had been reached which was to endure on the Western Front for more than three years. If the proponents of a neutral or a naval strategy had prevailed and Britain had not sent the BEF – or even if its departure had been delayed while a new government was formed – the German chances of victory over France would without question have been enhanced.

The Kaiser's European Union

That Britain could have limited its involvement in a continental war is a possibility historians have all but ignored. Even those who deplore the *way* the war was fought generally neglect this counter-factual. Yet it should now be clear that the possibility was a very real one. Asquith and Grey themselves later acknowledged this in their memoirs. Both men emphasized that Britain had not been obliged to intervene by any kind of contractual obligation to France. In Asquith's words, 'We kept ourselves free to decide, when the occasion arose, whether we should or should not go to war.' Nor did Grey make any secret of the political opposition within his own party which had prevented him making a commitment to France in July. Despite his talk elsewhere of irresistible historical forces, he admitted that there had been a choice.

Of course, Grey naturally insisted that the Cabinet's choice had been the right one. But what were his arguments *against* neutrality? In his memoirs, he set these out:

If we were to come in at all, let us be thankful that we did it at once – it was better so, better for our good name, better for a favourable result, than if we had tried to keep out and then found ourselves . . . compelled to go in . . . [Had we not come in] we should have been isolated; we should have had no friend in the world; no one would have hoped or feared anything from us, or thought our friendship worth having. We should have been discredited . . . held to have played an inglorious part. We should have been hated.

For Grey, then, the war was at root 'a matter of honour': the legal commitment to Belgium and, even more, the moral commitment to France. Nevertheless, the desire not to be cast as 'perfidious Albion' was only the veneer behind which strategic calculations lay. Grey's fundamental argument was that Britain could not risk a German victory, because such a victory would have made Germany 'supreme over all the Continent of Europe and Asia Minor'.

But was that really the German objective? Was the Kaiser really Napoleon? The answer to that question depends, of course, on what one thinks Germany's war aims actually were in 1914. According to Fischer and his pupils they were every bit as radical as the British Germanophobes feared. The war was an attempt 'to realize Germany's political ambitions, which may be summed up as German hegemony over Europe' through annexations of French, Belgian and possibly Russian territory, the founding of a

Central European customs union and the creation of new Polish and Baltic states directly or indirectly under German control. In addition, Germany was to acquire new territory in Africa, so that her colonial possessions could be consolidated as a continuous Central African area. There was also to be a concerted effort to break up the British and Russian empires through fomenting revolutions.

Yet there is a fundamental flaw in Fischer's reasoning which too many historians have let pass. It is the assumption that Germany's aims as stated after the war had begun were the same as German aims beforehand. Thus Bethmann's 'September Programme' – 'provisional notes for the direction of our policy' for a separate peace with France, drafted on the assumption of a swift German victory in the West – is sometimes portrayed as if it were the first overt statement of aims which had existed before the outbreak of war. If this were true, then the argument that war was avoidable would collapse; for it is clear that no British government could have accepted the territorial and political terms which the September Programme proposed for France and Belgium, as these would indeed have realized the 'Napoleonic nightmare' by giving Germany control of the Belgian coast. But the inescapable fact is that no evidence has ever been found by Fischer and his pupils that these objectives existed *before* Britain's entry into the war. It is in theory possible that they were never committed to paper, or that the relevant documents were

destroyed or lost, and that those involved subsequently lied rather than concede legitimacy to the
'war guilt' clause of the Versailles treaty. But it seems
unlikely. All that Fischer can produce are the pre-war
pipedreams of a few Pan-Germans and businessmen,
none of which had any official status, as well as the
occasional bellicose utterances of the Kaiser, an individual whose influence over policy was neither
consistent nor as great as he himself believed. It is of
course true that the Kaiser occasionally fantasized
about 'a sort of Napoleonic supremacy', and that,
when it belatedly dawned on him on 30 July that
Britain would intervene, he gave vent to the wildest
of global designs:

Our consuls in Turkey and India, agents etc., must fire the
whole Mohammedan world to fierce rebellion against this
hated, lying, conscienceless nation of shop-keepers; for if
we are to be bled to death, England shall at least lose India.

Moltke too envisaged 'attempts . . . to instigate an
uprising in India, if England takes a stand as our
opponent. The same thing should be attempted in
Egypt, also in the Dominion of South Africa.' But
such flights of fancy – worthy of John Buchan's
wartime thriller *Greenmantle*, and as realistic – should
not be seen as serious German war aims. Before the
war the Kaiser was just as prone to remind British
diplomats: 'We fought side by side a hundred years
ago. I want our two nations to stand together again

in front of the Belgian monument at Waterloo.' This was hardly Napoleonic talk. It is also of interest that as early as 30 July the Kaiser expected war with Britain to 'bleed Germany dry'. Indeed, even when the Kaiser did compare himself with Napoleon, it was with the Emperor's ultimate fate in mind: 'Either the German flag will fly over the fortifications of the Bosphorus', he declared in 1913, 'or I shall suffer the same sad fate as the great exile on the island of St Helena.'

The critical point is that had Britain not intervened immediately, Germany's war aims would have been significantly different from those in the September Programme. Bethmann's statement to Goschen of 29 July 1914 shows that he was prepared to guarantee the territorial integrity of both France and Belgium (as well as Holland) in return for British neutrality. Moltke's notorious 'Suggestions of a military–political nature' of 2 August said the same: the assurance that Germany 'would act with moderation in case of a victory over France . . . should be given . . . unconditionally and in the most binding form', along with guarantees of the integrity of Belgium. Had Britain in fact stayed out, it would have been foolish to have reneged on such a bargain. So Germany's aims would almost certainly not have included the territorial changes envisaged in the September Programme (except perhaps those relating to Luxembourg, in which Britain had no interest); they certainly would not have included the proposals for German control of the Belgian coast, which no British government could have tolerated. The most that would have remained, then, would have been the following proposals:

1. *France* . . . A war indemnity to be paid in instalments; it must be high enough to prevent France from spending any considerable sums on armaments in the next 15–20 years. Furthermore: a commercial treaty which makes France economically dependent on Germany [and] secures the French market for our exports . . . This treaty must secure for us financial and industrial freedom of movement in France in such fashion that German enterprises can no longer receive different treatment from French.
2. . . . We must create a *central European economic association* through common customs treaties, to include France, Belgium, Holland, Denmark, Austria–Hungary, Poland, and perhaps Italy, Sweden and Norway. This association will not have any common constitutional supreme authority and all its members will be formally equal, but in practice will be under German leadership and must stabilise Germany's economic dominance over *Mitteleuropa*.
[3.] *The question of colonial acquisitions*, where the first aim is the creation of a continuous Central African colonial empire, will be considered later, as will that of the aims realised *vis-à-vis* Russia . . .
4. *Holland*. It will have to be considered by what means and methods Holland can be brought into closer relationship with the German Empire. In view of the Dutch

character, this closer relationship must leave them free
of any feeling of compulsion, must alter nothing in the
Dutch way of life, and must also subject them to no
new military obligations. Holland, then, must be left
independent in externals, but be made internally
dependent on us. Possibly one might consider an offensive and defensive alliance, to cover the colonies; in any
case a close customs association . . .

To these points – in effect, the September Programme
without annexations from France and Belgium –
should be added the detailed plans subsequently
drawn up to 'thrust [Russia] back as far as possible
from Germany's eastern frontier and [break] her
domination over the non-Russian vassal peoples'.
These envisaged the creation of a new Polish state
(joined to Habsburg Galicia) and the cession of the
Baltic provinces (which would either be independent, incorporated in the new Poland or annexed by
Germany itself). Even this edited version of the
September Programme probably exaggerates the
pre-war aims of the German leadership. Prince
Bülow, of course, was no longer Chancellor; but his
comments on the subject in 1908 were not so different from Bethmann's view that war would
strengthen the political left and weaken the Reich
internally:

No war in Europe can bring us much. There would be
nothing for us to gain in the conquest of fresh Slav or

French territory. If we annex small countries to the Empire we shall only strengthen those centrifugal elements which, alas, are never wanting in Germany . . . Every great war is followed by a period of Liberalism, since a people demands compensation for the sacrifices and effort war has entailed.

Would the limited war aims outlined above have posed a direct threat to British interests? Did they imply a Napoleonic strategy? Hardly. All the economic clauses of the September Programme implied was the creation – some eighty years early, it might be said – of a German-dominated European customs union. Indeed, many of the official statements on the subject have a striking contemporary resonance: for example, Hans Delbrück's, that 'only a Europe which forms a single customs unit . . . can meet with sufficient power the over-mighty productive resources of the trans-atlantic world'; or Gustav Müller's enthusiastic call for a 'United States of Europe' (a phrase used before the war by the Kaiser) 'including Switzerland, the Netherlands, the Scandinavian states, Belgium, France, even Spain and Portugal and, *via* Austria-Hungary, also Rumania, Bulgaria and Turkey'; or Baron Ludwig von Falkenhausen's aspiration to:

match the great, closed economic bodies of the United States, the British and the Russian empires with an equally solid economic bloc representing all European states . . . under German leadership, with the twofold purpose:

1. of assuring the members of this whole, particularly Germany, mastery of the European market, and
2. of being able to lead the entire economic strength of allied Europe into the field, as a unified force, in the struggle with those world powers over the conditions of the admission of each to the markets of the other.

Even some of the German 'scaremongers' of the prewar period had argued in these strangely familiar terms. In *The Collapse of the Old World*, 'Seestern' (Ferdinand Grauthoff) had declared prophetically: 'The *union* of the European peoples alone can win back for them the undisputed political power and the dominion of the seas that they have lost. Today the centre of political gravity is in Washington, St Petersburg, and Tokyo.' Karl Bleibtreu's *Offensive Invasion against England* concludes: 'Only a peacefully united Europe can maintain itself against the growing strength of other races and against the economic domination of America. Unite! Unite! Unite!'

To be sure, Bethmann and Riezler had no doubt that this 'Middle European Empire of the German Nation' was merely 'the European disguise of our will to power.' Bethmann's aim, as Riezler put it in March 1917, was:

to lead the German Reich which by the methods of the Prussian territorial state . . . cannot become a world power . . . to an imperialism of the European form, to organize the Continent from the centre outward (Austria, Poland, Belgium) around our tacit leadership.

That is not the way German politicians talk today. But even put like that, Germany's European project was not one with which Britain, with her maritime empire intact, could not have lived.

Of course, it was not to be; the bid for British neutrality was, as we know, rejected. Yet historians have been too quick to dismiss Bethmann's proposal as wild miscalculation, or even to argue that the Germans themselves did not expect to secure British neutrality. The evidence does not bear this out. On the contrary, it shows that Bethmann's calculations were far from unreasonable. He can be forgiven for not anticipating that, at the very last minute, the arguments of Grey and Churchill would prevail over the numerically stronger non-interventionists; and that the majority of Members of Parliament would accept what would prove to be the Foreign Secretary's most misleading assertion: 'If we are engaged in war, we shall suffer but little more than we shall suffer even if we stand aside.'

POCKET PENGUINS

36. **Muriel Spark** The Snobs
37. **Steven Pinker** Hotheads
38. **Tony Harrison** Under the Clock
39. **John Updike** Three Trips
40. **Will Self** Design Faults in the Volvo 760 Turbo
41. **H. G. Wells** The Country of the Blind
42. **Noam Chomsky** Doctrines and Visions
43. **Jamie Oliver** Something for the Weekend
44. **Virginia Woolf** Street Haunting
45. **Zadie Smith** Martha and Hanwell
46. **John Mortimer** The Scales of Justice
47. **F. Scott Fitzgerald** The Diamond as Big as the Ritz
48. **Roger McGough** The State of Poetry
49. **Ian Kershaw** Death in the Bunker
50. **Gabriel García Márquez** Seventeen Poisoned Englishmen
51. **Steven Runciman** The Assault on Jerusalem
52. **Sue Townsend** The Queen in Hell Close
53. **Primo Levi** Iron Potassium Nickel
54. **Alistair Cooke** Letters from Four Seasons
55. **William Boyd** Protobiography
56. **Robert Graves** Caligula
57. **Melissa Bank** The Worst Thing a Suburban Girl Could Imagine
58. **Truman Capote** My Side of the Matter
59. **David Lodge** Scenes of Academic Life
60. **Anton Chekhov** The Kiss
61. **Claire Tomalin** Young Bysshe
62. **David Cannadine** The Aristocratic Adventurer
63. **P. G. Wodehouse** Jeeves and the Impending Doom
64. **Franz Kafka** The Great Wall of China
65. **Dave Eggers** Short Short Stories
66. **Evelyn Waugh** The Coronation of Haile Selassie
67. **Pat Barker** War Talk
68. **Jonathan Coe** 9th & 13th
69. **John Steinbeck** Murder
70. **Alain de Botton** On Seeing and Noticing